SACRAMENTO PUBLIC LIBRARY
828 "I" STREET
SACRAMENTO, CA 95814
9/2015

D0957044

An edge of ice split off and dropped into the deep dark hole. Hillary fell. He tried to slow himself by jamming his boots into the icy wall.

"Tenzing!" he shouted. "Tenzing!"

In a flash, Tenzing plunged his ice ax into the snow. He wrapped his rope around the ax to hold it steady. Then he threw himself on the ground, to anchor the rope even more.

The rope tightened. Hillary jerked to a stop. He was fifteen feet down, far into the crack of ice. Bit by bit, he pulled himself up. His gloves were torn, and his body was bruised. But he was alive.

The most exciting, most inspiring,
most unbelievable stories . . .
are the ones that really happened!

*The $25,000 Flight*
*Apollo 13*
*Babe Ruth and the Baseball Curse*
*Balto and the Great Race*
*Climbing Everest*
*The Curse of King Tut's Mummy*
*Finding the First T. Rex*
*The Race Around the World*
*The Titanic Sinks!*

# TOTALLY TRUE adventures!

# CLIMBING EVEREST

**How heroes reached
Earth's highest peak . . .**

by Gail Herman • illustrated by Michele Amatrula

A STEPPING STONE BOOK™

Random House 🏠 New York

Text copyright © 2015 by Gail Herman
Cover art and interior illustrations copyright © 2015 by Michele Amatrula
Photograph credits: title page © che/CC-BY-2.5; p. 3 © Rdevany/Wikimedia Commons/CC-BY-SA-3.0/GFDI; p. 19 courtesy of Ocrambo/Wikimedia Commons; p. 95 some rights reserved by Göran Höglund (Kartläsarn); p. 97 some rights reserved by Sam Hawley; p. 98 some rights reserved by simonsimages; p. 99 some rights reserved by Jonathan Keelty; p. 105 © Uwe Gille/Wikimedia Commons/CC-BY-SA-3.0/GFDL

All rights reserved. Published in the United States by Random House Children's Books, a division of Penguin Random House LLC, New York.

Random House and the colophon are registered trademarks and A Stepping Stone Book and the colophon are trademarks of Penguin Random House LLC.

Visit us on the Web!
SteppingStonesBooks.com
randomhousekids.com

Educators and librarians, for a variety of teaching tools,
visit us at RHTeachersLibrarians.com

Library of Congress Cataloging-in-Publication Data is available upon request.

ISBN 978-0-553-50986-1 (trade) — ISBN 978-0-553-50987-8 (lib. bdg.) —
ISBN 978-0-553-50988-5 (ebook)

Printed in the United States of America
10 9 8 7 6 5 4 3 2 1

This book has been officially leveled by using the F&P Text Level Gradient™ Leveling System.

Random House Children's Books supports the First Amendment and celebrates the right to read.

# Contents

# The Highest Challenge

How far would you go for adventure?

Centuries ago, explorers went thousands of miles. They crossed oceans. They blazed trails through forests and jungles. They wanted to discover places no one had seen. By the early 1900s, there weren't many new places left. Explorers had covered almost every corner of the world.

In 1909, explorers even reached the North Pole. In 1911, others conquered the South Pole. "Now what?" some wondered. What would be the next great challenge?

To find their answer, explorers looked up. Their thoughts turned to Asia and to the tallest mountain range on Earth, the Himalayas. This chain of mountains has the highest peak of all. It is on the border between Tibet and Nepal. Some call it the third pole.

Mount Everest.

In the mid-1800s, an Indian and British team measured Everest's height. They used a giant instrument called a theodolite. The height amazed them: 29,002 feet. The measurement was very close to what we know it is today: 29,035 feet. It was almost twice as tall as the Rocky Mountains.

Everest was officially the highest place on Earth.

No one had tried to climb its highest points. Not even the Sherpas, the people who lived in its shadow, had aimed for the top.

"Sherpa" means "people from the East." The Sherpas first settled around Everest more than

400 years ago. To get there, they trekked over mountain passes from Tibet to Nepal. They carried everything they owned on their backs. They built villages right into the sides of steep foothills. Their homes stood on ground higher than most mountaintops in the United States.

Sherpas called their mountain Chomolungma. Some say the name means "mother goddess of the

world." But to the Sherpas, it means "the mountain so high, no bird can fly over it." In other parts of Nepal, it is called Sagarmatha, which means "head of the sky" or "ocean mother."

As for "Everest," that name honors Sir George Everest. He was in charge of mapping and measuring the Himalayas.

But by any name, Mount Everest stands apart from all other peaks. And by the 1900s, getting to its top became every explorer's dream.

But could they survive the climb?

These men would have to tackle deadly weather in almost every season. Each year in the Himalayas, heavy, heavy rains fall between June and September. These are the monsoons, sudden storms that change the land. Bare, dusty ground turns into green grassy fields. Trees, bushes, and flowers grow. But monsoons bring flooding, too. And high in the mountains, the rain becomes snow, many feet deep.

The top of Everest, called the summit, is always very cold. Even in summer, the temperature hovers around zero degrees. In winter months, it can feel as low as seventy-five degrees below zero, matching the coldest temperatures in the Arctic. The worst winds on Everest are more than twice as strong as a hurricane. They can blow a person right off the mountain.

In the early 1900s, climbers could only imagine the dangers. But they'd reached the summit of the famous Matterhorn in the Swiss Alps. They'd climbed mountains in South America and in Alaska. They knew how to climb in ice and snow.

These men used axes to cut into ice and make steps. They roped themselves together, by tying one long rope around their waists. That way if one climber fell, the others could stop him from dropping farther. To keep each climber even safer, a partner wrapped the rope around a rock or an ax.

They knew the dangers. The higher they climbed, the colder and windier it would get. The air would grow thinner, and breathing would be harder. No one had climbed higher than 24,600 feet. Everest's summit was thousands of feet higher.

The risks didn't stop there. Would there be more avalanches so high up?

An avalanche is a great pile of snow that slides down a mountain. The snow gathers speed. And it grows bigger as it falls. It can sweep climbers down slopes and bury everything in its way.

And what about crevasses?

A crack in the ice, called a crevasse, could suddenly open under a climber's feet. He would fall down . . . down . . . into a gaping hole and, most likely, to his death.

Climbers knew they could get frostbite and lose feeling in parts of their body. They could be blinded by the sun shining on snow. Thin air could leave them tired and sick, hurt, confused, or worse.

But some climbers lived for those challenges. And one of those men was George Leigh Mallory.

## 2

# Mallory, the Man

George Leigh Mallory was born June 18, 1886. His family lived in a small village in England. The land was mostly flat. But that didn't stop Mallory from climbing.

Almost as soon as he could walk, Mallory scrambled up trees, drainpipes, and anything else he could find. He never worried about getting down. He just wanted to reach the top.

Mallory was always on the lookout for adventure. He had a way of making things fun and exciting—even dangerous. When he heard something was impossible, he only wanted to do it more.

When Mallory was seven years old, his parents got mad at him. They sent him to his room. He went, but just long enough to get his hat. Then he snuck outside and climbed onto the roof of the village church.

Not long after, Mallory and his family went to the beach. He was curious about the tide, so he climbed a large rock by the ocean's edge. Soon water surrounded the rock. Mallory wasn't scared. He was too busy looking around.

The water rose higher and higher. Mallory stayed on the rock, calm and quiet. Finally, his grandmother called for help. A man in a rowboat saved Mallory. The man said that the young boy hadn't been worried at all!

Mallory never grew out of that curiosity. He loved to take risks. At fourteen years old, he was a friendly, talkative teenager. One of his teachers taught him to mountain-climb. He loved it right away. Soon he was tackling some of the tallest mountains in Europe.

As Mallory got older, he became known as a skilled mountaineer. He was one of the best. He could take on climbs that no one else would. He found his way around huge rocks with ease. And he could pull himself up tall mountain cliffs, no matter how high.

Mallory was a man of action. He was good at acting fast—sometimes too fast. On one trip, he started a climb but forgot the safety rope.

Mallory was also a thinker. He wanted to make a difference in the world. So he became a teacher. He didn't get the chance to teach for long. World War I broke out.

Mallory watched his students leave school to fight. Some lost their lives. He couldn't just sit back. So at age twenty-nine, he joined the army. He had a wife and baby by then. It was hard to be away from them. And he learned hard lessons about life and death. When he came home, he wanted to make the most of his time. He didn't want to waste a precious moment.

He wanted more adventure.

Then, in 1921, Mallory got a letter from two big British climbing groups. Would he like to join an expedition to explore Mount Everest?

# 3

# 1921 Expedition: Exploring the Unknown

Today, there are many ways to climb Everest. The north side approaches from Tibet. The south side, from Nepal. To Mallory, it didn't make much difference. He didn't know what either side was like. But in 1921, only the north was open to climbers. So the British got permission from Tibet to climb Mount Everest.

This first expedition was called a reconnaissance (rih-KAH-nuh-zunts). It meant that the

team would explore and map out a trail. Mallory was supposed to learn about the area. But he also hoped he could try for the summit.

He didn't like to leave his wife, Ruth, or his growing family. But this was the chance of a lifetime.

First, Mallory took a boat to India. Then he rode a train to a city called Darjeeling. There he met up with nine British climbers. They would all walk north into Tibet together. The march

would be long and hard, and would last for months. They would be far away from shops, towns, and people. They needed food and equipment to last the entire time.

The supplies were too much for the men to carry. And pack mules could only go so high. So along with a few cooks, the British hired about forty porters to help. Porters carry baggage and other loads for people.

These porters were mostly Sherpas from

Everest villages. But their relationship with the British had started even before the Everest expeditions.

For many years, Sherpas had traveled to Darjeeling, looking for work. They went during the monsoon season, when heavy rains made it impossible to farm. These men had grown up in the mountains, walking up and down hills, carrying heavy loads. They took jobs building houses and roads, which demanded strength. The British living in India trusted them completely.

The Everest team left in the middle of May. Some men rode horses for the long trip. Mallory walked. He wanted to get used to the thin air and train for the climb. The Sherpas walked, too. They carried heavy boxes and baskets on their backs. Head straps made the loads feel lighter.

The men passed through misty jungles, then higher into forests of flowers. In early June, they reached Tibet and its dry, windy plains. Step by step, the group kept marching higher.

One month passed. Mallory saw smaller peaks through thick clouds, but he still hadn't spied Everest.

Finally, "the miracle happened," he wrote later to a friend. "Higher in the sky than imagination had dared to suggest, the white summit of Everest appeared."

The great mountain was still one hundred miles away. But Mallory felt a growing excitement. They were about to "walk off the map," he said in a letter to his wife.

As they came closer, Mallory saw more and more of Everest. It was connected to other peaks by lower mountain passes. The passes are called cols.

The North Col was the closer of the two. It would be Mallory's key to Everest. He knew if they tried to go straight up, the climb might be too steep. Instead, they would go around the base and up the col. It would be a longer climb, but an easier one.

Now they just had to find a way to the North Col!

In late June, they entered the Rongbuk Valley. The valley had been carved out by a glacier. A glacier is a large mass of ice that forms alongside mountains. It's like a sloping, frozen river. And, like rivers, glaciers flow and move. They carry dirt and rocks as they go, and shape land into valleys.

The giant Rongbuk Glacier snaked for miles around smaller glaciers and peaks. At its end, down a straight, long, and wide path, stood Everest.

It was just sixteen miles away. But it seemed impossible to reach. Its North Col was blocked by a hundred-foot wall of snow and ice.

The team pitched camp at 16,500 feet, on a sandy gravel floor. They weren't far from the

famous Rongbuk Monastery, a Buddhist place of worship. Sherpas, and many other people from the region, followed the Buddhist religion. The monastery, the highest in the world, was a place for them to think and pray. People traveled for days and weeks to visit. The paths of the monastery were lined with stones, and the stones had prayers carved into them.

When the British visited, several hundred religious men, called lamas, were staying there. Some Buddhists lived in nearby caves, spending time alone in quiet thought.

Back at its base camp, the expedition had a full view of Everest. The air was thin. The sun glared brightly, but it was getting colder.

The British had packed as if they were back home going on a climb. They had brought woolen slacks and suit jackets, raincoats, knit sweaters, scarves, hats, and hobnailed boots. The boots had nails hammered into the bottom, to better grip the snow.

These clothes were perfect for a day out in the English countryside. But they looked a little silly in the snowy peaks of the Himalayas.

The climbers had little protection against the dangers of Everest. Even so, the real search for the way up the North Col would begin.

Climbers from the team went up the mountain

in pairs. Partners helped each other fix ropes and stay safe. For four weeks, Mallory and Guy Bullock, his partner, scrambled around towers of ice that looked like castles. They climbed around forests of pointy ice sculptures and giant blocks of ice. Everything was colored an eerie shade of blue.

*It's like a fairyland,* Mallory thought.

The climbers would go up a bit and then back down. Each time they'd climb a little higher than before. This helped them get used to the height and the effects of thin air.

Usually, Mallory and Bullock were tied together for safety. They used their axes to cut steps in the icy slopes. When the ground was flat, the axes became good walking sticks.

Finally, in mid-August, they discovered the East Rongbuk Glacier. It led straight up to the col, then onto the top slopes of Everest.

"We have found out the way," Mallory wrote to his wife.

It took weeks to set up camp and move up the glacier. Still, the team thought they could make it to the top before bad weather really set in.

They decided to keep going. They would try to reach the top, just as Mallory had hoped.

In early September, he led a group from their

camp at 22,350 feet. They pushed through deep snow and reached the North Col. The summit was closer than ever.

But the temperature fell below zero. Violent winds swirled snow in every direction. Icy blasts pushed them back. Mallory and his men couldn't go on in this blizzard. The expedition was over.

For seven months, Mallory had been away from home. He'd missed Ruth and the children terribly. And for what? He hadn't come close to reaching the top. He felt like a failure.

But three months later, Mallory had another chance. A second expedition was headed for Everest. Mallory had found a way to the summit. He wanted to be the one to complete the climb. How could he say no?

# 4

# 1922 Expedition: Avalanche!

The 1922 expedition was better prepared. They had stronger climbers and more porters and Sherpas. They even brought cases of champagne. They could celebrate their success once they reached the top.

Even more important, they had a new plan. They would go straight to the East Rongbuk Glacier by a shorter path through the valley. Then they'd set up five or so camps. Each one would be higher than the last. From there they would go along the col, and, hopefully, to the summit.

For about a month, Sherpas took food and other supplies up to the camps. After each trip, they returned to the lowest camp to rest.

The climbers trekked up and down, too. They needed to get used to the thinner air and stay fit. Messengers carried letters and notes from camp to camp and into the nearest village to be mailed.

Soon climbers had to answer a new question. For the first time, the expedition had oxygen bottles. Climbers could wear masks and hook them up to the bottles. They would be able to breathe oxygen. But should they use the system?

Some climbers thought so. Clearly, extra oxygen would help in the thin air.

Others were against it. They thought it was like cheating. It would be unfair to Everest in the man-against-mountain contest. At first, Mallory was against it, too. He didn't like the idea of wearing a rubber mask while he climbed.

So on May 20, without oxygen, Mallory led a

group up from the col. They set up a high camp at 25,000 feet. This was a summit attempt. At last, Mallory would step onto the highest slopes of Mount Everest, where no one had gone before.

At eight o'clock the next morning, Mallory and two other climbers left their tent. Up so high, they moved very, very slowly. They could only travel 300 feet, about the length of a football field, each hour. It would take them more than

ten hours to reach the summit. They would be too late to return before dark.

At 26,800 feet, they were in a place called the Death Zone. The thin air and harsh cold made it very hard to survive. If climbers came here too fast from lower heights, they could die in moments.

Mallory and his men wouldn't last for long. They had to turn around.

A few days later, another summit team left.

This team carried oxygen. They turned back, too, at 27,235 feet. Still, they'd gone higher than Mallory, and their try changed his mind. Now Mallory believed oxygen was necessary to reach the top.

It was already early June. The monsoons, with their heavy snows, could arrive any moment. Was there time for another attempt?

Mallory wondered if it was too risky to go up again. "But how can I be out of the hunt?" he wrote to Ruth.

He decided to try.

Along with a group of British climbers, Mallory led fourteen Sherpas up into the North Col. He was careful. The men were separated into four groups. Each group roped themselves together. The British climbing team led the way. The Sherpas, with their loads, followed behind them.

Mallory knew there were dangerous spots. Avalanches were likely where fresh snow had fallen. He carefully tested each step. Finally, he thought they were past any danger.

Suddenly, Mallory heard a sharp sound, like an explosion. A huge mass of snow slid right at them! It pulled Mallory down the mountain. Another thick wave covered him completely. Mallory moved his arms as if he were swimming. He struggled out. He gasped for air and looked around.

The men on his rope were all fine. But what about the Sherpas below? They must have been hit even harder!

Mallory peered down the mountain. Five Sherpas rose to their feet. But two ropes of Sherpas had been swept over an ice cliff. They had fallen sixty feet.

Mallory and the others rushed to help. They pulled two men out of the snow. But seven were lost. The first people to die climbing Everest were Sherpas.

The expedition ended quickly. Mallory blamed himself for the deaths. He had acted without thinking, just as he had when he was a child. He should have realized the danger, he thought. "The consequences of my mistake are so terrible," he wrote to a friend. "It seems impossible to believe that it has happened."

Now he knew climbing Mount Everest wasn't only an adventure. It was life or death.

# 5

# 1924 Expedition: Mallory's Final Climb

Mallory grew even more serious about reaching the summit. Men had lost their lives on Everest's slopes. But he wanted to reach the goal he had set.

Over the past two years, he'd been away from home for long stretches of time. He missed his family. He wanted to be with them. But he couldn't give up the struggle.

In early 1924, Mallory gave a talk in New

York City. A reporter asked, "Why do you climb Mount Everest?"

His famous reply: "Because it is there."

For Mallory, that was all there was to it. When he was invited on the 1924 expedition, his answer was yes.

In the end, his wife understood his decision. According to family legend, Mallory promised to leave a photograph of Ruth on the summit. Still, good-byes weren't easy. Mallory's third child, John, was only three years old when he left.

The 1924 group was a mix of old team members and new ones. Mallory was now the climbing leader. He wanted Andrew "Sandy" Irvine for a partner. He liked the twenty-two-year-old student right away. Irvine wasn't an experienced climber. But he was young, strong, and daring. He also knew a lot about oxygen bottles and how to fix them if anything went wrong.

When they got to base camp, everyone

celebrated with a five-course dinner. But troubles came quickly. While setting up camps, they were hit by blizzard after blizzard. One team member died suddenly, most likely from being in the thin air. Others had frostbite, lung infections, and broken bones. Even Sherpas suffered from being so high up. Many got headaches and started vomiting. Almost everyone had altitude sickness.

Already, the expedition had lost precious time. Something had to be done to lift the team's spirits.

Edward Norton, the leader of the entire expedition, went to the Rongbuk Monastery. He asked the head lama to give a special blessing to the Sherpas.

Instead, the lama invited all the climbers to the monastery. Everyone trooped the four miles from base camp.

The British gave the lama a gift. Then he held a silver prayer wheel to each man's head. By doing this, he gave the climbers a blessing.

As the lama sat on a red throne, the team gathered around. Demons had held them back before, he said. They would try to do so again. The men must be strong. He would pray for them.

Everyone felt better. They returned to work. And soon the first pair to try for the summit set

off. They moved up Everest from camp to camp.

On June 4, Norton and his partner, Howard Somervell, left camp 6. The camp was just one tent, on the North Col of the mountain, at 26,700 feet. From there, they moved slowly along a band of yellow rock. The path would take them to the northeast ridge that led to the summit.

The two men were climbing without oxygen. Right away, they felt tired and sick. The air was so thin, they could only take ten steps at a time. Then they had to rest. They bent over, hands on knees, panting hard. Every five minutes they sat down for a break.

Somervell was suffering from a cough. In the dry air, his cough got worse. It rattled every bone in his body. At 28,000 feet, he told Norton to go on without him.

Norton struggled on. But he was in terrible shape, too. Just before a narrow ridge, he'd taken off his goggles. He wanted to see the way more clearly. But the sun made the snow shine very brightly. Its harsh glare became more and more powerful. The strong light hurt Norton's eyes. Soon he was seeing double.

Still, Norton kept climbing along a deep gorge. It was hard to keep his balance. He felt as if he were climbing a steep roof with slippery shingles.

Then, at 28,126 feet, Norton stopped. His eyesight was so blurry, he could barely see. Every step was full of danger.

Somehow, he stumbled back to Somervell. They started down together. Somervell fell behind. Then he began to choke. His throat was blocked and frozen, and he couldn't breathe. He couldn't even call out to Norton. He could only sink into the snow, thinking this was the end.

But Somervell gathered his strength. He made a fist of both hands and thumped his chest. This unblocked his throat.

Somervell and Norton barely made it back to

camp. By then Somervell was completely "snow-blind." It would take days for him to see clearly.

In the meantime, Mallory got his oxygen ready. He and Irvine would try next.

Throughout the weeks at Everest, Mallory wrote letters by lamplight. He wrote to his daughters about having tea parties and to his wife about missing her. He read poetry and played cards with his teammates.

And now it was all nearing an end. On June 6, he and Irvine left camp 4 with a group of Sherpas.

Mallory wore goggles and an air force helmet. He carried twenty-eight pounds.

The group climbed up to camp 5. Some of the Sherpas returned to lower camp, with a note from Mallory: "There is no wind here, and things look hopeful."

The next day, Mallory led the team higher up to camp 6. There, the rest of the Sherpas turned back, too. They delivered another note from

Mallory: "We'll probably start early tomorrow (8th) in order to have clear weather."

The try for the summit was on.

Early the next morning, team member Noel Odell climbed toward camp 6. He wanted to help Mallory and Irvine as they came down.

Sleet and snow began to fall. A fast-moving mist quickly covered the slopes. Odell couldn't see much. At 26,000 feet, he paused. Where were Mallory and Irvine?

He climbed to a higher point to get a better view. Then, just before 1 p.m., the mist lifted. He could see the upper slope of Everest.

Two rock steps hung like cliffs just below the summit. And there, somewhere near the steps, Odell spied one black dot. A climber!

Another dot moved closer to the first. Mallory and Irvine! They were moving steadily toward the top. But they were hours behind schedule.

Then, just as suddenly, the mist dropped again. The dots disappeared.

Odell went back to camp 6 to wait for the climbers, just as a snowstorm hit. When the sky cleared, Odell left to look for his teammates. Did Mallory and Irvine climb to the summit? Or did they turn around in the storm? In either case, they might have lost their way.

Odell shouted. He whistled. He yodeled. He peered in all directions. Nothing. He searched in the Death Zone that day and the next, struggling in the thin air. He even climbed as high as 28,000 feet.

He waited. Then he waited some more.

*It's no use,* he thought. *They must have lost their lives.*

At camp 6, Odell pulled out the sleeping bags. He placed them in a T-shape. It would be a sign to the others farther down the mountain. Mallory and Irvine were gone. Dead, without a trace.

The news traveled quickly. Friends, family, and climbers were in shock. Mourning bells rang across England.

The expedition ended with sadness and mystery. What had happened to the climbers? Did Mallory and Irvine fail? Or did they reach the summit?

# 6

# Sherpa Tenzing Norgay

Sherpas from the failed expedition returned home. Most of them lived in the Khumbu Valley in Nepal, in the shadow of Everest.

In one village called Thamey, a young boy listened to the Sherpas' stories. His name was Tenzing Norgay. In 1924, Tenzing was around ten years old. He had always been fascinated by the mountain. He could listen to Everest tales for hours. But he had chores. There was much to do.

Tenzing's days were much like his ancestors'. Sherpas usually didn't go to school. Tenzing's village didn't have one. There were no stores or hospitals. There were no roads to the outside world—just narrow, winding trails.

His family farmed a small plot of land near their stone house. Animals crowded into the bottom story of the house. Tenzing and his parents, brothers, and sisters climbed a ladder to the second floor, where they all shared a room.

The family rose at dawn and worked hard. They never went hungry, but sometimes they struggled. The climate was harsh. It was cold and frosty in the winters, and hot and rainy in the summers. The land was rocky. Only potatoes grew easily.

Other boys played games with mud and rocks and ran around the village. But Tenzing was shy and kept to himself. He herded the family yaks high up on the slopes. Alone, he'd climb as high as 18,000 feet. He stopped only when he got to a place so high, it was too cold for grass to grow.

From here, he could clearly see Everest. He called it the Sherpa name, Chomolungma.

Tenzing never grew tired of staring at the peak and its snowy summit. He was curious, but also a little scared. His Buddhist religion taught him that gods and demons lived in the mountains. They were sacred places, to worship and to protect.

They were not places to climb, Tenzing knew. And he realized the danger. Men had died climbing Everest.

Still, Tenzing dreamed about going even higher on Everest's slopes. He wondered what it was like, so close to the sky.

Why scramble up mountains? his family would ask, laughing. What good would it do? Tenzing should stop daydreaming, they said. He should tend to the land and the yaks.

But Tenzing couldn't stop thinking about the Sherpas who left his village for Everest. He was fascinated by the British, too. *Chillingna,* he called them, "men from faraway places." They were exploring Everest! It seemed unbelievable!

*What is it like to climb so high?* he wondered.

Some Sherpas had brought back heavy climbing boots. Tenzing tried them on. He could barely walk.

But Tenzing knew he was young. He'd just

wait until he was bigger and stronger. Then he could wear those boots. Then he could join the British when they explored Everest. He'd see for himself what it was like at the top of Chomolungma.

7

# Tiger of Everest

Years passed. Tenzing left home to live and work in India. In 1935, he went to the British Tea Planters Club in Darjeeling. The twenty-year-old stood in a long line of Sherpas. The men were all looking for porter jobs.

These men knew about the 1922 avalanche that killed seven Sherpas. They knew that Mallory and Irvine had died on the mountain, too. Still, Tenzing and the other Sherpas waited. They hoped to be hired for the next Everest expedition.

In one climbing season, they could earn more than they could by farming all year long. They'd have enough money to buy land. Maybe enough to hire Sherpas to carry their own loads!

On a platform above the men, expedition leaders looked up and down the line. Some of these Sherpas had been on expeditions before. They carried a list of all their climbing trips, and had letters of recommendation from other Western climbers.

Tenzing didn't have any experience. He didn't have a book. He didn't even have the traditional Sherpa hairstyle, one long braid down his back. British teams looked for the braid as a sign of Sherpa strength and skill. Tenzing had cut it off when he first came to Darjeeling.

But he did have a brand-new jacket and khaki shorts. And, excited by the thought of climbing, he had a great big smile.

A famous climber named Eric Shipton asked

Tenzing to step out of line. Disappointed, Tenzing turned to leave. He felt sure he hadn't gotten the job. But Shipton saw something special in Tenzing. He hired him on the spot.

This was Tenzing's first Everest expedition, and the fifth for the British. The team began the usual trek through India to Tibet, then on to Everest.

Everything about the English seemed strange to Tenzing. He had never worn goggles or used small cooking stoves to melt snow for water. He had never seen food in tin cans or sleeping bags.

But Tenzing learned quickly. He grew to understand British customs and got the hang of mountaineering. He cut steps in the ice with an ax, used a rope, and scouted paths in the snow. More than anything, Tenzing wanted to be a Tiger. This was an honor given to Sherpas who reached the highest heights.

Finally, the expedition reached the Rongbuk

Valley. And there was Everest! It was hard for Tenzing to believe, but his old village was on the other side of the mountain, just a few miles away.

On this 1935 expedition, Tenzing climbed to 22,000 feet. He carried ninety pounds of supplies. High on the North Col, he set up camp, cooked, and worked hard. He was on his way to becoming a true Tiger.

But there was no try for the summit. The monsoons had arrived.

The other Sherpas happily started back down. They had no interest in climbing higher or exploring Everest at all. Carrying loads up the mountain was only a job. It was a way to earn money and provide for their families.

Tenzing realized that he was different. For him, climbing Everest meant more than a paycheck. He wanted to keep pushing up its slopes. He wanted to look down from a high perch onto the valleys below.

"It is a dream," Tenzing later wrote in his autobiography. "A need, a fever in the blood."

During the next seventeen years, Tenzing returned to Everest again and again. He worked on almost every expedition, large and small. He even became a Tiger. But every time, the men failed to reach the top.

In 1952, Tenzing joined a Swiss expedition as Sherpa leader. He was part of the climbing team, too. But for the first time, the group wouldn't approach from Tibet.

The world had been going through changes. Now no one from the outside could visit Tibet. Meanwhile, Nepal was welcoming visitors. So the Swiss—and Tenzing—were going to climb up the south side.

As with the northern path through Tibet, the expedition started with a march. Tenzing met the group in Kathmandu, the capital of Nepal. They traveled 180 miles through the Khumbu region, where Tenzing grew up. The weather was warm. Sherpas wore shorts as they carried their heavy loads. The team walked through deep valleys and over high ridges, past almond trees and colorful flowers.

Sometimes they crossed roaring rivers on narrow plank bridges. After sixteen days, they reached the large, bustling village of Namche Bazar.

Meanwhile, Tenzing's mother had been walking, too. She traveled from her village of Thamey to Namche Bazar to see her son.

"Here I am at last!" Tenzing cried. It had been eighteen years since they had seen each other.

The British expeditions had been visiting the Rongbuk Monastery before every climb. Now the Swiss continued the tradition in Nepal.

They visited the Tengboche Monastery, at 12,000 feet, and stopped for tea. From there, they could see Everest straight ahead. The mountains

Lhotse and Nuptse stood on either side.

Then they climbed more than 4,000 feet to set up base camp. They were on the edge of the Khumbu Glacier. It is one of the highest glaciers in the world.

Tenzing felt comfortable with the climbers. He liked one in particular, Raymond Lambert. Lambert had lost all his toes to frostbite on another climb. He had to wear special boots now, but that didn't stop him from trying to get to the summit. Tenzing understood.

The two teamed up for the summit try. They reached 28,250 feet, the highest point ever. They were only 1,000 feet from the top.

Tenzing and Lambert tried again in the fall. But deadly winds forced them off the mountain once more. It was a bitter blow.

Would anyone ever be able to climb to the summit?

## 8

# Hillary Grows Up

That spring, while Tenzing and Lambert were on Everest, a climber named Edmund Hillary was in another part of the Himalayas. He waited eagerly for news of their expedition.

Then he heard: the Swiss had failed. Mount Everest was still undefeated.

Hillary had all sorts of feelings about the news. He admired the Swiss and was sorry they didn't make it. But he also felt a growing excitement.

Hillary had explored Everest before. He knew

he'd be going back. And maybe, just maybe, he would be the first to reach the summit.

Edmund Hillary was born in Auckland, New Zealand, on July 20, 1919. He grew up in a small farming town outside the city. He never even saw a mountain until he was sixteen years old.

His family didn't travel far from home. They were busy keeping cows and growing fruits and vegetables. But their main business was bee-keeping. They had 1,600 hives!

Hillary spent his days having picnics by a nearby river, building rafts, and having fun. He'd imagine a stick was a sword and have great pre-tend adventures.

At night, his father told stories about a made-up character called Jimmy Job. Jimmy Job fought evil and faced danger at every turn. Hillary loved these stories. But he loved true adventure tales even better. His favorite was the story of George

Mallory and the Everest expeditions.

Hillary's elementary school had only three rooms. Students of all ages mixed together. As a young boy, Hillary was small, skinny, and shy. He had few friends. But he was very smart and graduated early.

Hillary started his next school at age eleven. He was younger than the other students and still scrawny. He felt out of place. A gym teacher made the situation even worse. He placed Hillary in a special gym class. It was a place for "misfits," Hillary thought.

Hillary didn't like school much at all. Yet each morning he rode his bike to the train station to take an early train. He wouldn't get home until after six.

They were long days. But Hillary liked the train rides.

Sometimes he'd leap off the train as it started. Then he'd grab on to a handle and run next to it

as it picked up speed. Finally, he'd swing back inside.

Hillary loved to run. He had more energy than most boys. And he was growing, too, taller and stronger. He was also learning to box.

But the highlight of those years came at age sixteen, when he took a school trip to New Zealand's Mount Ruapehu.

It was Hillary's first mountain and his first glimpse of snow. It was all so new! Nothing could be better than to be outdoors and active in this exciting, new world.

When Hillary went to college, he ran the five miles between home and school. He joined a "tramping" club, too, and went on hike after hike. He also kept growing. In his late teens, Hillary stood almost six and a half feet tall. But one thing hadn't changed. He still didn't like school.

Hillary was practical. He knew his grades were poor. And he knew he had a job at home. So he left college to become a full-time beekeeper. He liked being outside and getting exercise. Working with bees almost felt like an adventure.

Hillary was busy, but he still took time to hike. When he was twenty, he visited Mount Cook National Park. At a lodge, he overheard two men. They talked about climbing to the top of Mount Cook, the highest peak in New Zealand.

Mountain climbing! Like Mallory! Hillary remembered the stories he loved as a boy. *I should be climbing, too,* he thought. The very next day, he set out to climb a nearby peak. And he reached the summit! From then on, he went to the mountains as often as possible.

Meanwhile, World War II was starting. Hillary didn't believe in fighting, or like the idea of war. But the battles came closer to home. In the end, he joined New Zealand's air force.

For the first time, Hillary traveled out of the country. He discovered that there was much to see in the world, both good and bad. He was curious. Maybe mountain climbing would be his ticket to adventure. He looked to the Himalayas.

In June of 1951, Hillary got an invitation from Eric Shipton. Shipton wanted Hillary to join a British team exploring Everest. Their plan was to map the south side, from Nepal.

The team explored the lower slopes. They discovered a path to the summit. But the Swiss were climbing next. Hillary had to wait two years to return.

And then his Himalayan adventures really began.

# 9

# The 1953 Expedition Begins

In 1953, the British organized another expedition. They were going to climb the south side of Everest. And they invited Edmund Hillary and Tenzing Norgay to join their group.

Tenzing hesitated. Of course he wanted to try to reach the summit again. But he wanted to climb with his friend Raymond Lambert.

Tenzing was almost thirty-nine now. He had a wife and children. Tenzing knew he wouldn't get another chance. He'd be too old. He agreed to go.

On March 1, Tenzing gathered his Sherpa team. Then he packed for one last expedition. He carried two special items: a small red-and-blue pencil from his daughter and a red scarf from Raymond Lambert.

The Sherpas met the British team in Nepal. The group included two New Zealanders, Hillary and his friend George Lowe. Even before they were introduced, Hillary recognized Tenzing. He had heard all about Tenzing's skill and daring on Everest. And the Sherpa had a "quiet air of confidence."

For the first part of their journey, 350 porters from Nepal carried 473 cases of supplies. Many of these porters were women. They were so strong, they could hold the loads *and* babies at the same time.

The team traveled into the mountains and arrived at the Tengboche Monastery. There, the expedition camped for several weeks. The climbers trained on low peaks and got used to the thin air. Light snow covered the ground in the mornings. But the days grew warm and sunny.

By mid-April, they set off again, following the Khumbu Glacier. Soon they crossed the snow line. After this imaginary line, the temperature would stay below freezing. There would be only ice and snow and rock. No trees, bushes, or grass could survive.

The expedition trekked over heaps of stone and soil left behind by the glacier. They walked between huge ice towers. They jumped over freezing-cold streams and followed paths of ice.

When they reached a flat rocky spot circled by pointy columns of ice, they stopped. This would be base camp. And there was much to do. Hundreds of people went to work. They pitched tents, unpacked supplies, and sorted food.

A radio system to talk with higher camps was set up. So was a post office for mail. It was like a small city, where people slept, ate, read, talked, listened to the radio, and even got haircuts.

At almost 18,000 feet, the men breathed in about half as much oxygen as they would at sea level. They could hear creaks and cracks as the ice moved and shifted.

From the earlier expedition, Hillary knew the next test they had to tackle: the Khumbu Icefall. The icefall was higher up the glacier. It looked like a frozen waterfall with ice blocks the size

of houses. It demanded true skill to climb. The ground trembled and shook. Holes opened and closed without warning. It could be deadly.

Hillary's heart sank when he saw it. The path he knew from his first expedition was gone.

Icefalls, like glaciers, move and change. Crumbling ice towers and deep cracks now blocked the way. Snow and ice made bridges across some crevasses. These "bridges" would have to be tested carefully.

Still, the icefall had to be climbed. And not just once, but many times, to carry supplies up to higher camps. The Sherpas were in charge of these heavy loads. For them, the climb would be doubly difficult. A new, safe route had to be found.

Hillary volunteered for the job. Perhaps John Hunt, the expedition leader, would like his work. Then maybe he would choose Hillary for a summit team. Only two pairs would try for the top. More than anything, Hillary wanted to be one of the climbers. First, he had to prove himself.

## 18

# Summit Team

Hillary led a group of climbers up the icefall. He cut large steps in the ice with his ax. He made sure to make smaller ones for handholds, too. Climbing was easier now than it was in Mallory's time. Instead of hobnailed boots, the men wore crampons. These spikes strapped on to their boots and had a stronger grip.

Hillary's team used long pine poles and ladders to cross giant cracks. They placed ladders along steep ice cliffs, too. For each one, they fixed a rope to hold on to for balance. They nailed

the heavy cord into solid snow with pegs. And finally, they marked the path with flags. Hillary made sure everything was held down.

The team worked for days. They forced a path through the ice and pitched camp 2, midway up the icefall. Then they placed camp 3 at the top.

They had climbed about 2,300 feet from base camp. They were one-third of the way to Everest's peak. The men had reached the entrance to the Western Cwm, the next part of the climb.

A cwm, pronounced *coom,* is a bowl-shaped mountain valley. This one stretched for two and a half miles. It was surrounded by solid walls of rock. Its floor was cracked with crevasses. Some were eighty feet wide.

Inside the cwm, there was no wind, not even a breeze. The tall rocks blocked air currents. When the sun shone, the temperature climbed as high as ninety-five degrees. But it could drop below freezing in a matter of minutes.

To carve out a path on the cwm, Hillary teamed up with Tenzing for the first time. The two roped themselves together and set out. The sun beat down on them without mercy. It was deathly quiet.

When the men were done stamping out a trail, they climbed back down to camp 2. George Lowe was staying there overnight.

Hillary promised his friend he would call him when they reached base camp. Each day, radio calls from camp to camp went out at five o'clock.

Lowe laughed. Already, it was after four. No one had ever traveled that quickly from camp 2. "That'll be the day," he said.

A challenge! Hillary liked nothing better. He set off at a run, with Tenzing right behind. They hurried down through the lower icefall. Soon they came to a crevasse. Hillary didn't want to waste time crossing an ice bridge. Instead, he leapt across. He landed on the other side.

*Crack!*

An edge of ice split off and dropped into the deep dark hole. Hillary fell. He tried to slow himself by jamming his boots into the icy wall.

"Tenzing!" he shouted. "Tenzing!"

In a flash, Tenzing plunged his ice ax into the snow. He wrapped his rope around the ax to hold it steady. Then he threw himself on the ground, to anchor the rope even more.

The rope tightened. Hillary jerked to a stop.

He was fifteen feet down, far into the crack of ice. Bit by bit, he pulled himself up. His gloves were torn, and his body was bruised. But he was alive.

Hillary thanked Tenzing. He'd saved his life. But Tenzing didn't make a big deal about the rescue. It was all in a day's work.

The two continued down. Even with the accident, they made it to base camp just at five o'clock. Hillary grabbed the radio. He gasped "Hello" to Lowe.

He and Tenzing had broken the speed record for climbing down the icefall! But more important, Hillary realized they made a great team.

No one seemed stronger than Tenzing. Other men fell ill. They got sick working in the thin air. Or they grew too tired to keep going. Tenzing barely seemed to suffer as they climbed higher. Lambert had joked he had three lungs, because it seemed so easy for him to breathe.

Tenzing did have a trick: he kept moving. He

was always checking equipment, boiling water, and making sugared lemon juice. That way he kept his body warm and his mind clear.

For the next few days, the team worked to set up camps 4 and 5 in the cwm. Again, Hillary and Tenzing climbed together. They proved to John Hunt that they were strong and fit. He named them as one of the two summit teams.

Meanwhile, at the far end of the cwm, Lowe led a trailblazing group to a wall of sheer ice. It rose almost 4,000 feet, about the height of three Empire State Buildings.

This was the Lhotse Face. They would have to climb it to get to the South Col, which in turn led to the top slopes of Everest.

Lowe was in charge of ice-cutting. His group toiled for weeks. Storms hit. Work started and stopped. But finally, the team carved a path. They pitched camps 6 and 7 on small ledges of ice, then camp 8 on the South Col itself.

The col, at 25,800 feet, was just over 3,000 feet from the summit. It began the south side's Death Zone. This large flat area of rock was a bleak, icy place. Fierce, howling winds blew so strongly, snow couldn't stick to the ground. Climbers have called it the loneliest place on Earth.

By now it was the end of May. The monsoons were coming. Time was running out.

# 11

# In the Death Zone

On May 26, Charles Evans and Tom Bourdillon, the first summit team, started their climb from camp 8. Their goal was actually the South Summit, 335 feet below the top. If they felt it was safe to go on, then they would push for the highest summit of all.

They climbed to 28,700 feet, higher than anyone else before. But the pair had trouble with their oxygen bottles. It was too difficult to continue. They turned around at the lower summit.

Hillary was waiting at camp 8. He watched

the men return. They moved slowly, as if they wore cement boots. Every step was an effort. Both climbers were covered in ice from head to toe.

Hillary and Tenzing listened to the climbers describe their trek. The slopes were slippery, and snowy rocks hung right off the mountain. They discussed these problems and the dangers. If a tower of ice suddenly fell, it could crush the climbers. If they got tired and made a mistake, their next step could be their last.

Everyone would spend another cold night at camp 8. Then Hillary and Tenzing, the second team, would move forward. The two had a different plan for the summit push. They would set up one more camp higher on Everest and stay overnight. It would be the highest camp ever.

That night, a storm raged for hours. The temperature dropped to thirteen below. The wind roared, shaking the tent from top to bottom. It was a sleepless night. And the next day started out no better. Tenzing and Hillary would have to wait an extra day in the Death Zone.

On May 28, Tenzing and Hillary, with Lowe and their support team, left for camp 9. Each climber carried about fifty pounds. It was a huge burden this high up. Here, even fifteen pounds was a full load.

The team pushed on slowly. They were tired beyond belief. Each step needed focus. The icy slope was bare and hard. They had to kick the ice to dig in with crampons.

They climbed higher. Every so often, the group had to stop. They'd bend over to give their backs and lungs a chance to rest.

The climbers lost track of time. It seemed as if they had been doing this forever. By midafternoon, they stood at 27,900 feet. It was the site of their final camp.

It was hard for Tenzing and Hillary to say good-bye to Lowe and the others. Once their teammates returned to lower camps, Tenzing and Hillary were alone. They were too high up to use the radios. And there would be little chance of rescue if something went wrong.

Together, Tenzing and Hillary set up camp.

From this spot, they could look down on the other Himalayan peaks. In the fading light, they scraped away snow to form a small ledge. Then they labored to put up the tent. It would have been quick work anywhere else. Here it took hours.

When they were done, the tent stood on the edge of the South Face slope, with a sheer drop below.

Finally, they crept inside. Hillary took off his boots. He couldn't bear to put them back on his cold, aching feet. He knew the boots would be frozen in the morning, but he would deal with that later.

The climbers ate chicken noodle soup, biscuits, and sardines. They gulped down the sweet lemon drink. They talked a bit, pausing as great gusts of wind shook the tent. Tomorrow would be summit day.

## 12

# The Roof of the World

Throughout the night, Hillary and Tenzing slept with their oxygen bottles by their sides. Every few hours, they turned them on, then off, then on again.

At 3:30 a.m., they woke for good. The temperature was minus sixteen. *Not bad for this altitude,* Hillary thought. Still, the tent flaps had frozen shut, and his boots were stiff with ice. He held them over the hot stove for an hour before he could put them on.

At 6:30, the men crawled outside. They wore all

the clothes they'd brought, including three pairs of gloves, long woolen underwear, and two pairs of pants. Tenzing put on Lambert's red scarf.

Each carried thirty pounds of oxygen equipment.

Lastly, they tied on their rope and gripped their ice axes. It was time to go.

First Tenzing led, then Hillary. They climbed along the steep ridge. Only a thin layer of snow and ice covered the rock. At 9 a.m., they reached the South Summit and paused to clean their oxygen tubes.

Just 500 feet separated them from the top.

But then they came to a great rock wall, standing forty feet high. It was the last big challenge before the summit. Later, it would be called the Hillary Step.

Hillary peered closely at the wall, looking for a way up. Slowly, he squeezed into a narrow gap in the rocks. He pushed his crampons into one icy side and lifted himself up. He was breathing hard and moving at a snail's pace. Tenzing held him steady with the rope.

At the top, Hillary gasped. For the first time, he thought they might actually make it.

Tenzing started to go up next. Hillary pulled up the rope to help him climb.

Then they rested.

Mounds of snow hid the path ahead. It was impossible to see what lay beyond each one.

The two men cut ice steps. Then they cut more ice steps, and even more. They felt desperately tired. Yet they went on. They climbed over each mound, until they reached the end and saw only deep blue sky.

The summit!

Hillary stepped up onto the snowy dome. Tenzing followed a step behind. Both agreed that it didn't matter who got there first. "We reached the summit almost together," they later said.

It was 11:30 in the morning. The sun was shining. And Tenzing and Hillary stood on the roof of the world. They were up so high that they could see clouds beneath them.

Hillary reached for Tenzing's hand. They shook. Then Tenzing threw his arms around Hillary in a great big hug. They thumped each other on the back.

Hillary always thought things through. He got out his camera and took a photo of Tenzing. Now they had proof that they'd made it to the top. Tenzing posed with his ice ax. He'd wrapped flags from the United Nations, India, Nepal, and Great Britain around its handle.

Next, Hillary snapped photos of the views. The great Himalayas stretched in all directions.

Tenzing thought of his friend Raymond Lambert, who had come so close to sharing this moment.

Hillary felt "a quiet glow of satisfaction . . .

more powerful than I had ever felt on a mountain-top before."

Tenzing left gifts for the mountain gods—sweets, and the pencil his daughter had given him.

Then the climbers searched the slopes, hoping for signs of Mallory's and Irvine's bodies. They found nothing.

Fifteen minutes had passed. It was now time to go down.

Tenzing and Hillary didn't care about being famous. They climbed Mount Everest for themselves. Nothing more, nothing less. But after they came back, the whole world took notice. Front-page newspaper headlines shouted the news. Everest had been conquered! At last!

Hillary was knighted by the Queen of England. Tenzing received awards and medals from Nepal and India, and England, too. There were parades and parties. And Tenzing, who had never left the Himalayan region, traveled the world.

Everyone wanted to know about the first climbers to reach the summit of Mount Everest.

But were Tenzing and Hillary really the first? What about Mallory and Irvine?

## 13

# To the Top?

On May 1, 1999, thirty-five expedition teams were climbing Everest. All the teams were trying to reach the summit, except for one. It was the seventy-fifth anniversary of Mallory's final climb. And the Mallory and Irvine Research Expedition wanted to solve the mystery of 1924.

One member, Conrad Anker, spied something out of the ordinary. "A strange patch of white," he would later say. It wasn't snow. It wasn't rock. He took a closer look.

It was a body, a male, lying facedown in the

snow. His feet were pointed toward the mountain base. His arms were outstretched, as if trying to stop a fall. He had a broken leg, broken ribs, and a broken shoulder. He wore one hobnailed boot and torn, old-fashioned clothes.

The clothing had a name tag: G.L. MALLORY.

The team searched Mallory's pockets.

There were goggles. Did that mean he fell in the dark, at nighttime? If he had been out so late, did he reach the summit?

There were letters from family and friends in

his pockets, too. But there was no picture of Ruth.

Did he leave the photo on top of the mountain, as he'd promised?

Many believe the answer to both questions is yes. They believe Mallory would never have turned back without climbing to the top first.

"Because Mallory was Mallory," another climber explained. He would have kept going, in snow and wind and darkness, in pain and exhaustion, even if it meant death.

Irvine's body is still missing. So is the expedition camera. Maybe it holds more clues, or even photos taken from the summit.

In the end, no one knows for sure what happened. But Mallory and Irvine, along with Tenzing and Hillary, have inspired thousands to try that same climb. To reach the top of Everest.

Today, in fact, hundreds climb Everest each year. The view is the same as it's always been. But much has changed.

In Nepal, an airport in the Khumbu region is named after Hillary and Tenzing. In Tibet, there are paved roads. Cars bring climbers straight to base camp. North- and south-side base camps have the Internet and cell phones. Trash is littered around Everest's slopes. There are empty oxygen bottles, sleeping bags, tent parts, and more.

Many Sherpas have given up farming. Instead, they work in the tourist industry. They try to balance Sherpa traditions with the ways of the modern world. Buddhist prayer flags fly at every base camp, and expeditions still visit the monasteries.

Expeditions guide dozens of groups every climbing season. Each climber pays anywhere from $30,000 to $120,000. Some are expert mountain climbers. Others have no experience at all.

Now that climbers have better tools and know the paths, reaching the summit is easier. But the risks haven't changed. In fact, with so many people on the mountain, there are added dangers. The crowding means long waits on fixed ropes. People stuck in lines so high up get tired, confused, and clumsy. Add this to sudden storms, plus ice and snow hazards, and more lives than ever can be lost.

The climbing Sherpas have paid the price more than any other group. In April 2014, sixteen Sherpas died in an avalanche. They were fixing ropes on the Khumbu Icefall so that climbers would have a clear and safe path.

Like the Sherpas and porters of Mallory's and Hillary's times, these people work to support their families as best they can. And some, like Tenzing and so many others, dream of reaching the highest point on earth.

Why?

Because it is there.

Turn the page for more amazing facts!

# THE STORY BEHIND THE STORY

## CLIMBING EVEREST

### In Their Fathers' Footsteps

Edmund Hillary and Tenzing Norgay reached the top of Mount Everest in 1953. Almost fifty years later, the families met on Everest again. Hillary's son, Peter, and Tenzing's son Jamling joined an expedition to celebrate the fiftieth anniversary.

Jamling had already climbed to the summit in 1996. That was a tragic climbing season. While he was on the mountain, eight people died in a blizzard. Jamling did what he could to help. He promised his wife he would never climb again. But in 2002, he stayed at base camp to head up climbing team communication.

Peter had already reached the top, too. That year, he decided to try again. The winds grew stronger and stronger as Peter and the team went up. In the end, they only had time for one try. Peter called it "a last-ditch effort at the end of the season." But they made it! The climb was another triumph for both families.

BASE CAMP AND RONGBUK MONASTERY

# Yeti: Fact or Fiction?

For thousands of years, people of the Himalayas have told stories of a strange creature called the yeti, or abominable snowman. The giant half-man, half-animal is covered in fur and is said to roam the mountains. He walks on two legs and swings his arms like an ape. He has extraordinary powers: great strength and the ability to fly.

Some believe the yeti is more than legend, though. Climbers have seen dark, hulking shapes in the distance. Unusual footprints have been found, some by Eric Shipton and Edmund Hillary. In 2012, a British scientist tested "yeti" hair. The samples matched a bone from an ancient polar bear. So the yeti may very well be real. It could be the relative of this prehistoric bear, and a strange creature found nowhere else on Earth!

# After Everest

Edmund Hillary's adventures didn't stop after he climbed Everest. He explored the North and South Poles! One expedition was with Neil Armstrong, the first man to walk on the moon.

Still, Hillary's heart belonged to the Himalayas. He felt a deep connection to the Sherpas. They had helped him reach his dream, and he wanted to help them, too. He asked one Sherpa what his people needed most. The answer: schools for their children.

STUDENTS FROM PANGBOCHE PRIMARY SCHOOL, WHICH WAS STARTED BY EDMUND HILLARY

So in 1961, Hillary planned and built the Khumjung School. It was the very first school for Sherpas. And it was blessed by the same lama who blessed Hillary's 1953 expedition. More schools followed, along with hospitals and bridges.

Hillary helped connect the Sherpas to the world. But he didn't want the people to lose their culture. He worked to establish Sagarmatha National Park around Everest and to rebuild the Tengboche Monastery after it burned down.

TENGBOCHE
MONASTERY

STATUE OF
EDMUND HILLARY

All the while, Hillary lived in Sherpa homes and became part of their families. Tenzing traveled the world, then settled in India to start his own climbing company. When Tenzing died in 1986, Hillary was there to pay his respects. He was part of the Sherpa community until his own death in 2008.

# Records on Everest

- **Fastest climb to the top:** May 21, 2004, twenty-six-year-old Pemba Dorje Sherpa, in eight hours and ten minutes from the south-side base camp
- **Most climbs to the top:** Apa Sherpa and Phurba Tashi Sherpa, twenty-one times each
- **Oldest man to reach the top:** eighty-year-old Yuichiro Miura of Japan, May 23, 2013
- **Oldest woman to reach the top:** seventy-three-year-old Tamae Watanabe of Japan, May 19, 2012
- **Youngest boy to reach the top:** thirteen-year-old Jordan Romero of the United States, May 22, 2010
- **Youngest girl to reach the top:** thirteen-year-old Malavath Poorna of India, May 25, 2014
- **Longest stay on the summit:** twenty-one hours, Babu Chhiri Sherpa of Nepal, May 1999
- **Most people to reach the summit on one day:** 234 on May 19, 2012
- **Most climber deaths in one season:** fifteen in 1996
- **Most Sherpa deaths in one season:** sixteen in just one day, April 18, 2014, in an avalanche

# Firsts on Everest

- **First to reach the top from the north side:** the Chinese team of Wang Fu-chou and Chu Yin-hua, and a Tibetan named Konbu, May 1960
- **First American to reach the top:** Jim Whittaker, May 1, 1963
- **First woman to reach the top:** Junko Tabei from Japan, May 16, 1975
- **First climb to the top without oxygen bottles:** Italian climber Reinhold Messner and Austrian climber Peter Habeler, May 8, 1978
- **First disabled climber to reach the top:** Tom Whittaker, May 27, 1998, using an artificial leg
- **First climber to snowboard all the way down from the summit:** Marco Siffredi from France, May 23, 2001. The next year, he tried again and disappeared.
- **First blind climber to reach the top:** American climber Erik Weihenmayer, May 25, 2001
- **First wedding on the summit:** bride Moni Mulepati and groom Pem Dorjee, both from Nepal, May 30, 2005

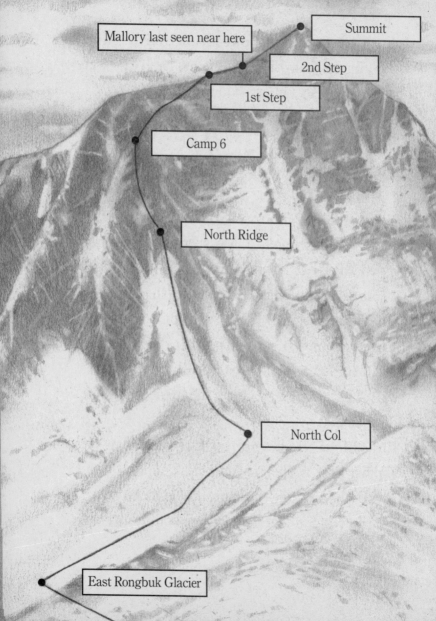

MALLORY'S ROUTE UP
THE NORTH SIDE

Summit

Mallory last seen near here

2nd Step

1st Step

Camp 6

North Ridge

North Col

East Rongbuk Glacier

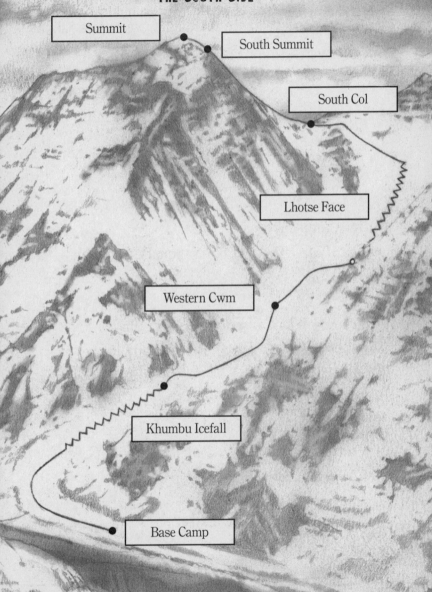

# Hillary/Tenzing's Route Up the South Side

Summit

South Summit

South Col

Lhotse Face

Western Cwm

Khumbu Icefall

Base Camp

# Further Resources

Here are a few more nonfiction resources about Mount Everest and its climbers:

## Documentaries

- *Everest* from IMAX
- *Everest: 50 Years on the Mountain* from National Geographic
- *The Man Who Skied Down Everest* from Image Entertainment
- *The Wildest Dream* from National Geographic

## Books

- *The Boy Who Conquered Everest: The Jordan Romero Story* by Jordan Romero with Katherine Blanc
- *Mystery on Everest: A Photobiography of George Mallory* by Audrey Salkeld
- *Triumph on Everest: A Photobiography of Sir Edmund Hillary* by Broughton Coburn

## Websites

- EverestNews.com
- nzedge.com/edmund-hillary
- pbs.org/wgbh/nova/everest

## About the Author

**G**AIL HERMAN has written many books for children, including several books in the Disney Fairies series. She has also written *Flower Girl, Otto the Cat, What a Hungry Puppy!, The Lion and the Mouse,* and *There Is a Town.*

# Get ready for more

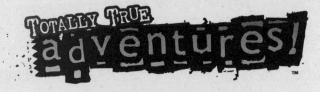

Nellie Bly had an amazing idea. What if she tried to go around the world in less than eighty days? In 1889, people said it could not be done—especially by a woman. But soon, the whole world was rooting for her! Could she make it back home in time?

*Available now!*